GCSE PERFORMANCE PIECES
PIANO

SERIES EDITOR: ANDREW S. COXON
COMPILED BY: JEREMY WARD

About the series editor **2**

About the author **2**

Introduction **3**

APOLOGIZE 4
MAD WORLD 10
THIS LOVE 14
LADY MADONNA 20
WALKING IN MEMPHIS 26
YOUR SONG 36
A THOUSAND MILES 43
SONG FOR GUY 50
THE WINNER TAKES IT ALL 58
HALO 68

ABOUT THE SERIES EDITOR

Andrew Coxon graduated from York University with a joint Honours Degree in Music and English before going on to Leeds University to complete a PGCE, and later gained a further degree through the Open University. He has had a teaching career spanning more than 40 years, for the most part as a Head of Department, and has been an examiner and moderator for many years, currently holding a senior GCSE examining position. He has recently authored music education materials for Rhinegold Education and Nelson Thornes.

Having spent most of his professional life in the North East, he now teaches part-time in Cumbria where he lives with his wife, son and a border collie. He still gains tremendous enjoyment from his classroom work, organising two instrumental groups and taking part in regular concerts, all in addition to his regular church organ-playing duties.

ABOUT THE AUTHOR

Jeremy Ward joined Rockschool as Director of Academic Affairs in 2002. He has been responsible for syllabus development across the portfolio and the company has grown substantially both nationally and internationally, now operating in over twenty countries outside of the United Kingdom. He was appointed Executive Director in 2011.

Jeremy began playing the piano at the age of four and half, and was successful in international competitions, taking first prize on two occasions. His love of rock and pop was always present and he has spent much of his time writing songs, improvising (gaining a second prize in international competition) and playing in bands with his brother, who plays the guitar.

Other titles in this series:
Flute, Clarinet, Alto Saxophone, Guitar, Bass Guitar, Drums, Voice

Rhinegold Education also publishes GCSE and A Level Study Guides, Listening Tests and Revision Guides for the Edexcel, AQA and OCR specifications.

First published 2012 in Great Britain by
Rhinegold Education
14-15 Berners Street
London W1T 3LJ
www.rhinegoldeducation.co.uk

© 2012 Rhinegold Education
a division of Music Sales Limited

All rights reserved. No part of this publication may be reproduced, stored in a retrieval system, or transmitted in any form or by any means, electronic, mechanical, photocopying, recording or otherwise, without the prior permission of Rhinegold Education.
Rhinegold Education has used its best efforts in preparing this guide. It does not assume, and hereby disclaims, any liability to any party for loss or damage caused by errors or omissions in the guide whether such errors or omissions result from negligence, accident or other cause.

GCSE Performance Pieces: Piano
Order No. RHG533
ISBN: 978-1-78038-635-5
Exclusive Distributors:
Music Sales Ltd
Distribution Centre, Newmarket Road
Bury St Edmunds, Suffolk IP33 3YB, UK

Edited by Ruth Power
CD recorded, mixed and mastered by Jonas Persson

Printed in the EU

Design by www.penguinboy.net

Images courtesy of Getty Images.

INTRODUCTION

This book offers ten pieces for you to play. They are at a range of standards, from the equivalent of Grade 3 through to Grade 6. However, as these pieces have not been set by any examination board thus far, grades are given as guides and you should ask your teacher to check with the GCSE examination board and/or its specification for a final ruling.

There is a mix of styles covering the period from 1968, with The Beatles' 'Lady Madonna', to Beyoncé's 'Halo', from 2008. The selection includes two songs by Elton John and the widely-known 'The Winner Takes It All' by ABBA. There may well be some songs which are less familiar to you but, if you are willing to spend time practising them, I am sure you will really enjoy them and gain great satisfaction from being able to play them well.

There's also a range of demands on your playing ability – for example, 'Mad World', originally by Tears for Fears, will allow you to demonstrate your skill at playing more slowly and lyrically, while Vanessa Carlton's 'A Thousand Miles' has a terrific piano riff for you to master.

The important thing to do when thinking about what to prepare for a performance examination is to choose something which is comfortably within your technical abilities. It is not a good idea to choose a piece on the basis that it is hard and will, therefore, gain you a higher mark for difficulty. This may be the case but, with any examination board, at GCSE it is your ability to play the notes and rhythms correctly, to show that you understand the style and character of the piece and to demonstrate that you can play it with total confidence and conviction that will gain you most marks. You are, after all, giving a musical performance and you would not want to go to a concert to hear very difficult songs played badly!

With each piece, there is expert advice on how to approach it, what you should look out for (for example, particular techniques you will need to master) and how to shape the piece into a really musical performance. Please read this through carefully before you start on any of the pieces and be prepared to refer back to it if you need to.

I am sure you will find plenty of music in this book to enjoy and will have great success playing the wide range of tunes.

Good luck!

Andrew Coxon
Series Editor

SUGGESTED LISTENING

A YouTube playlist has been created containing all the songs in this book for you to listen to. The playlist also contains any additional suggested listening the author recommends, including cover versions and wider listening to help you get a feel for each song and its cultural context. Listening to a wide range of music will help you create your own interpretation.

Access the playlist by searching YouTube for 'Rhinegold Education', where you'll find our channel and the playlist within it. Alternatively, scan this QR code with your smartphone to go straight there.

APOLOGIZE
ONEREPUBLIC
GRADE 3 STANDARD

OneRepublic

'Apologize' was the track that propelled rock band OneRepublic to international fame. Released in 2006, it peaked at Number 1 in 16 countries around the world and it remains their most popular song.

During your performance, the examiner will be looking for an immediate grasp of the pace and rock style. Make sure you use the first eight bars of the bands introduction to settle the speed. The intro is played staccato but after that the piano part is smooth. It is important that you play the right hand close to the keys to ensure you control the sound. It needs to be moderately quietly (***mp***) like a wash of sound rather than individual strikes of the chords. Your tone should be projected and confident. Make sure the upper note of the chord can be heard and therefore the movement from bar to bar. The left hand needs to be balanced with the lower note being more dominant. Use the pedal to help sustain the line.

SONG STATS
Tempo: ♩=122
Key Signature: 3 ♭s

At the chorus (bar 33), the dynamic needs to be loud (***f***) to show contrast with the verse, and there is a musical trick of moving the feeling of accent, in this case 3+3+2. This will work best if you hold the upper note a little longer than written and create a chord. Think of an accent on these notes to move the line along. Also watch the hand position for the stretches.

Make sure you play the slurred notes marked. These imitate the opening and will show the examiner your attention to stylistic detail. The rest at the bottom of the fourth page (bar 53) is crucial and it would be best to make it a little longer rather than shorter. It makes the following entry (bar 54) much more dramatic and the dynamic needs to be very loud (***ff***).

SUGGESTED LISTENING

Listen to the popular recording with Timbaland as well as the original recording of the band by themselves. Notice the difference in feel between the two versions and use these to create your own interpretation.

APOLOGIZE

Words & Music by Ryan Tedder
© Copyright 2005 Sony/ATV Tunes LLC/Velvet Hammer Music/Midnite Miracle Music.
Sony/ATV Music Publishing.
All Rights Reserved. International Copyright Secured.

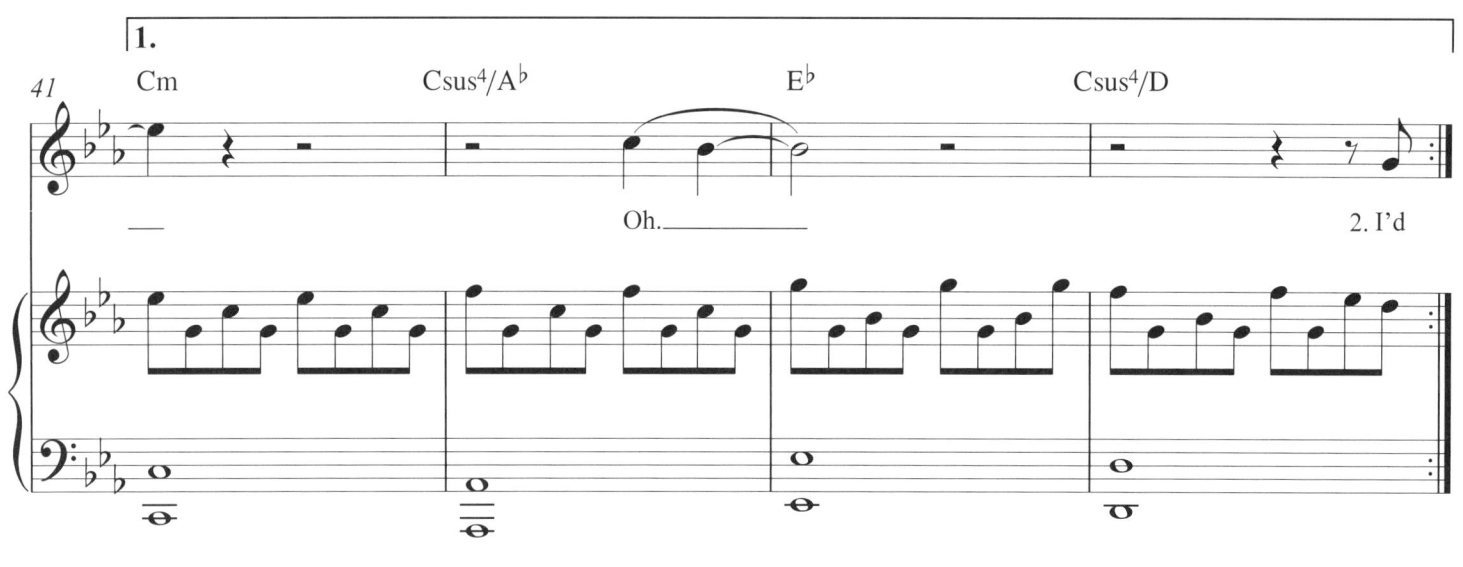

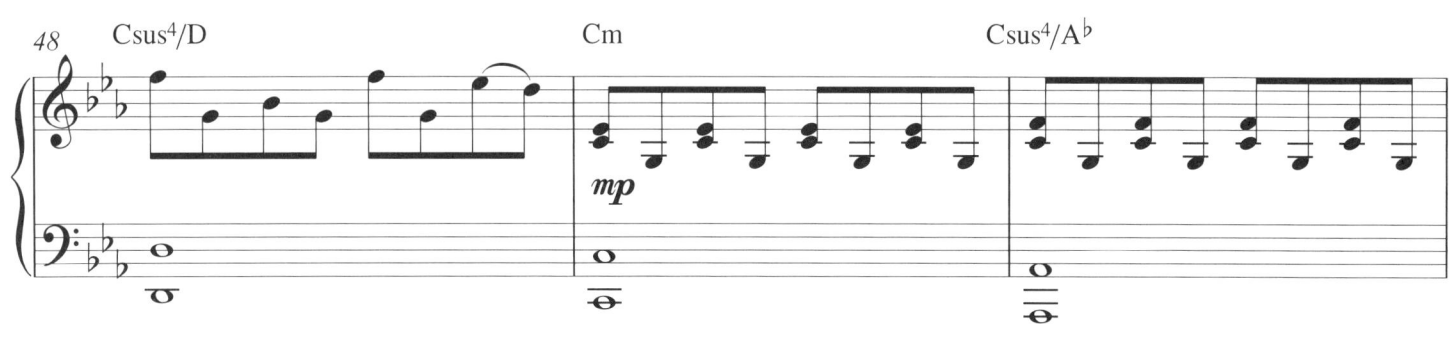
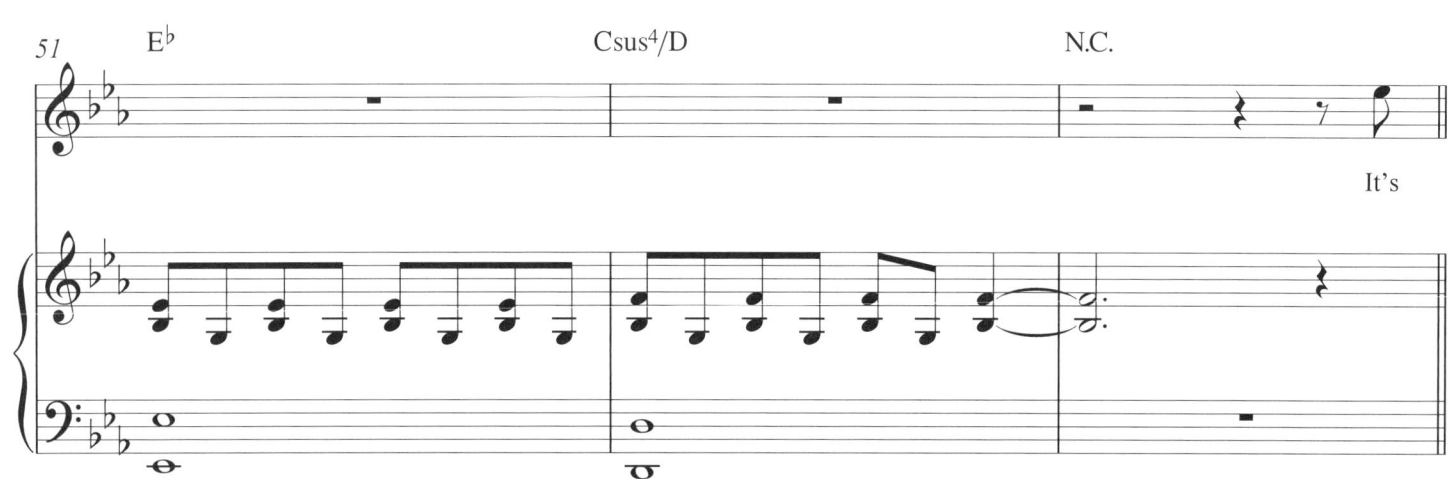

MAD WORLD
TEARS FOR FEARS
GRADE 3 STANDARD

Tears For Fears

'Mad World' was originally released in 1982 by the British band Tears for Fears before being rerecorded by Michael Andrews and Gary Jules in 2001 for the film *Donnie Darko*. This is the later version.

This is a good song to choose if you want to show off your more lyrical and slower playing. The piano starts so you have to be very sure of the pace. Be careful not to rush the opening descending phrase and make sure the dynamic is the marked moderately quiet (***mp***). The examiner will be looking for a warm and lyrical approach. Think of a decrescendo through the first bar and take care to observe the rests in the right hand in the second bar. Ensure that the left hand is not too loud or plodding. Play the notes close to the piano to ensure you control the tone and volume. Use of the pedal every half bar will help the line here.

SONG STATS

Tempo: ♩=88

Key Signature: 3 ♭s

The melody on the backing track is played on the guitar so you will have to play very quietly (***pp***) to make sure it can be heard. This is not easy as the piano register is low and therefore the sound is louder as the strings are thicker. Think about using the *una corda* (the soft pedal, generally the leftmost pedal on pianos) if you cannot hear the tune. Also make sure you give the notes good length and use the pedal here. For the second verse, you can be a little more inventive with the right hand, splitting the chords into single notes.

From bar 22 onwards, there is more movement in the right hand and the notes need to flow and sound as a phrase. The trick here is to listen to the volume after the tied note and to equal it rather than play it louder. If you can master this, it will be a musical and technical accomplishment.

From bar 29, there is the melody from the beginning but this time mixed between the two lines of the right hand. The examiner will be looking for you to be holding the upper notes here.

SUGGESTED LISTENING

Listen to the original Tears For Fears song, as well as the Andrews/Jules cover. Both have their own unique feel that you can use to base your own interpretation on.

MAD WORLD

THIS LOVE

MAROON 5
GRADE 3 STANDARD

Maroon 5

This song was written by the band Maroon 5 for their debut album *Songs for Jane* in 2002. It was the song that catapulted them to international stardom. Written about a romantic break-up, it is based around a strong piano strut that is immediately recognisable. The examiner will be looking for a confident and projected sound, played with authority and a degree of showmanship.

From the beginning, the strong left hand plays with the guitars and bass so practise just this with the backing. The dynamic needs to be loud (*f*). Make sure you get the rhythm correct before putting both hands together. The examiner will want to see that you don't shorten the last note of the bar. The right hand chords need to be played staccato and tightly, but watch you don't get faster as the riff progresses.

SONG STATS
Tempo: ♩=92
Key Signature: 3 ♭s

Just before the chorus (bar 16), the rhythm changes to include rests in the chords. Make sure you play these chords with a crescendo as it adds to the excitement of the chorus that follows. The long, sustained chorus chords need to be balanced and played with warmth and projection (*f*) and a strong left hand progression is needed. The examiner will be looking out for the tricky rhythm in bar 20 as this propels the line. Think of these notes as staccato.

On the repeat, the dynamic needs to be moderately quiet (*mp*) and the examiner will be listening to make sure you balance with the rhythm in the backing. The ending (from bar 47) requires right hand octaves in a falling figure. Ensure these are tidy and equal and make sure the left hand chords are given full length.

SUGGESTED LISTENING

Listen to the song and watch the band's dynamic performance in their promotional video. Try to put some of this energy into your own performance.

LADY MADONNA
THE BEATLES
GRADE 4 STANDARD

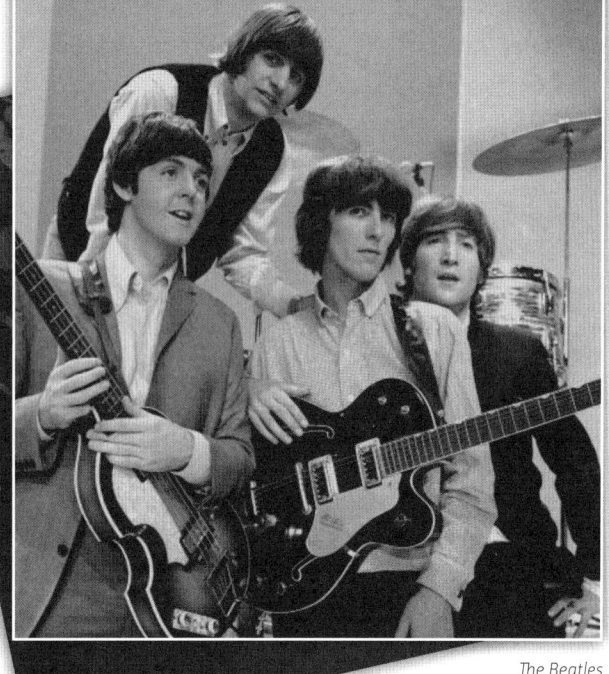
The Beatles

Written primarily by Paul McCartney (credited to Lennon and McCartney) for the Beatles in 1968, 'Lady Madonna' was the last track recorded for Parlophone Records. All subsequent work was recorded on their own label, Apple Records. The saxophone solo was originally played by the legendary Ronnie Scott.

This track relies heavily on a strong left hand technique. The octave work requires practice – look for the similar shapes. The examiner will be looking for detail such as a clear staccato on the upper note and a weighted, slightly longer lower note featured from bar 25.

The right hand needs to be controlled but bright in tone to achieve the style. The melody is in the lower part and so you need to ensure this can be heard clearly. Also make sure the rhythm in bar 1 (repeated throughout) is correct.

SONG STATS

Tempo: Moderately

Key signature: 3 #s

Where there are crotchets and minims, make sure they are given full length. The left hand pattern does alter for the verse (from bar 13), where the octave work requires a jump. Fingering is very important here. Make sure you notice the time signature change towards the end (bar 56).

SUGGESTED LISTENING

Listen to this classic song and get a sense for the infectious groove the piano is playing. Try to replicate the boogie-woogie feel in your performance.

LADY MADONNA

WALKING IN MEMPHIS
MARC COHN
GRADE 4 STANDARD

Marc Cohn

'Walking in Memphis' was written by American artist Marc Cohn for his album of the same name in 1991. The cover recorded by Cher for her 22nd studio album *It's a Man's World* is probably the most famous version.

The opening piano riff requires careful balance between the hands, particularly in the first bar and the examiner will be looking for a moderately loud dynamic. The pedal needs to be used here. Make sure you are confident of the pace from the outset. Fingering is also important to ensure fluency. Practise the movement of the thumb in the right hand to make sure you get there in time. A good thing to remember here is to travel across the keys and not move too high and far away from the note.

As this progresses, make sure you hold the tied notes for full value or you will begin to creep ahead of the track. Also make considerable use of the pedal to help hand positions. At the chorus, the movement moves to the left hand and there is some quite tricky interval work here (from bar 21). The secret is to ensure you move the 5th finger from the A at the end of the phrase to the F which is the beginning of the next phrase.

Make sure the right hand chords are balanced and the rhythms crisp. After this section, the work is predominantly left hand only and this requires care in control of pace and even articulation (from bar 28). Again, make sure the ties are given full value. You will need to balance with the backing track here and the examiner will be looking for evenness.

SONG STATS
Tempo: ♩=130

Key signature: No flats or sharps.

SUGGESTED LISTENING
Listen to both the original, and Cher's famous version to hear two different interpretations of this song.

In the middle section, there is some advanced rhythm work where there are half bar triplet rhythms in bar 54 followed by demisemiquavers in bar 58. Make sure these are spaced and controlled. This is meant to be the relaxed section before the restatement of the first theme. At bar 70. make sure you wait the full four count of the hi-hat in the backing track before coming back in.

To ensure a successful performance of this piece, you will need to have considerable technical control and evenness of tone.

WALKING IN MEMPHIS

Words & Music by Marc Cohn
© Copyright 1991 Sony/ATV Harmony.
All Rights Reserved. International Copyright Secured.

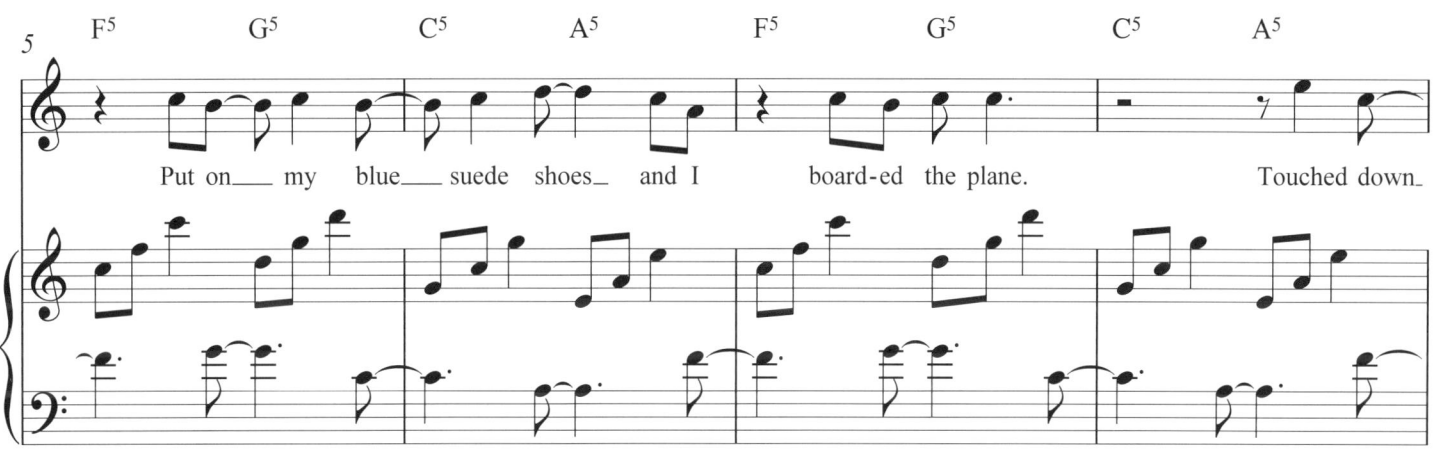

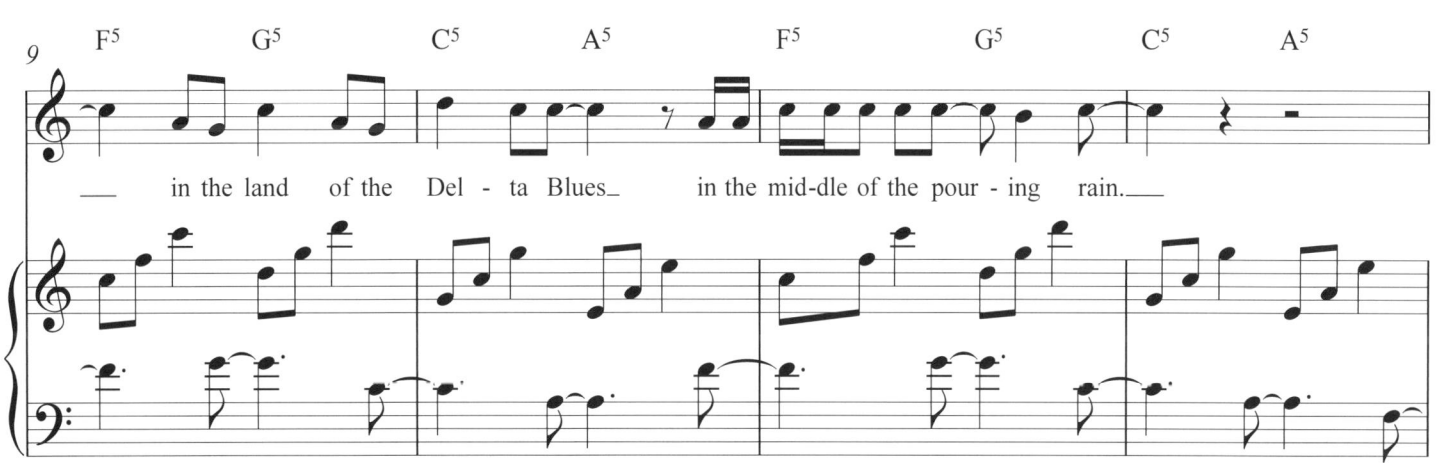

YOUR SONG
ELTON JOHN
GRADE 4 STANDARD

Elton John

'Your Song' was composed by Elton John and his lyric collaborator Bernie Taupin. It was released on Elton's eponymous album in 1970 and was his first commercially successful pop song. UK singer/songwriter Ellie Goulding recorded a stripped-back version of the song in 2010 which achieved considerable commercial success due to its inclusion on the John Lewis Christmas TV commercial.

The opening piano riff is instantly recognisable and requires a warm tone and even articulation. It is extremely important to use the pedal cleanly here.

Left hand notes must be supportive and given good value, and must not intrude into the right hand figure. At the verse, the riff is played in the warm, middle register of the piano. Be careful that the chord work is balanced and not given unnecessary accent (from bar 3).

Just before the middle eight watch out for the bar of 2/4 (at bar 20). The middle eight itself uses a popular technique of subdividing beats into 3+3+2 (bar 21). Octaves are on the first of these subdivisions and move up in step. Be sure this is brought out as it creates a degree of tension and forward movement. Make sure that the left hand minims are correct in length and supportive. There are quite a few time changes in this section so take care.

SONG STATS

Performance directions: Flowing

Tempo: Allegro Moderato ♩=124

Key signature: 3 ♭s

SUGGESTED LISTENING

There are many different cover versions of this song, but perhaps the most famous recently is by Ellie Goulding. Listen to this for a softer take on the song.

YOUR SONG

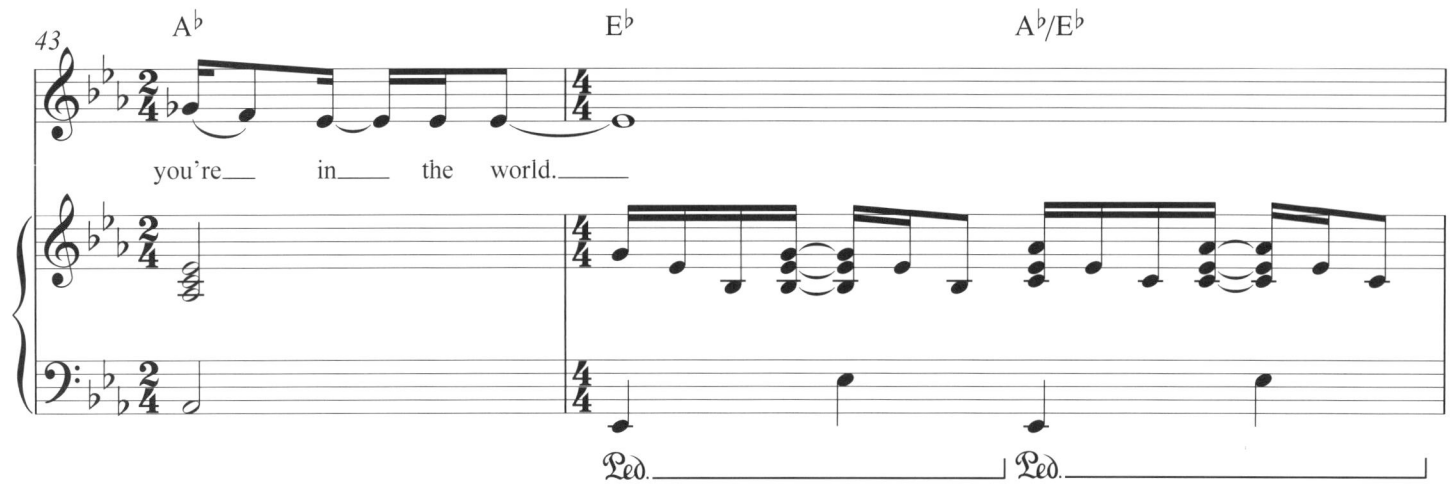
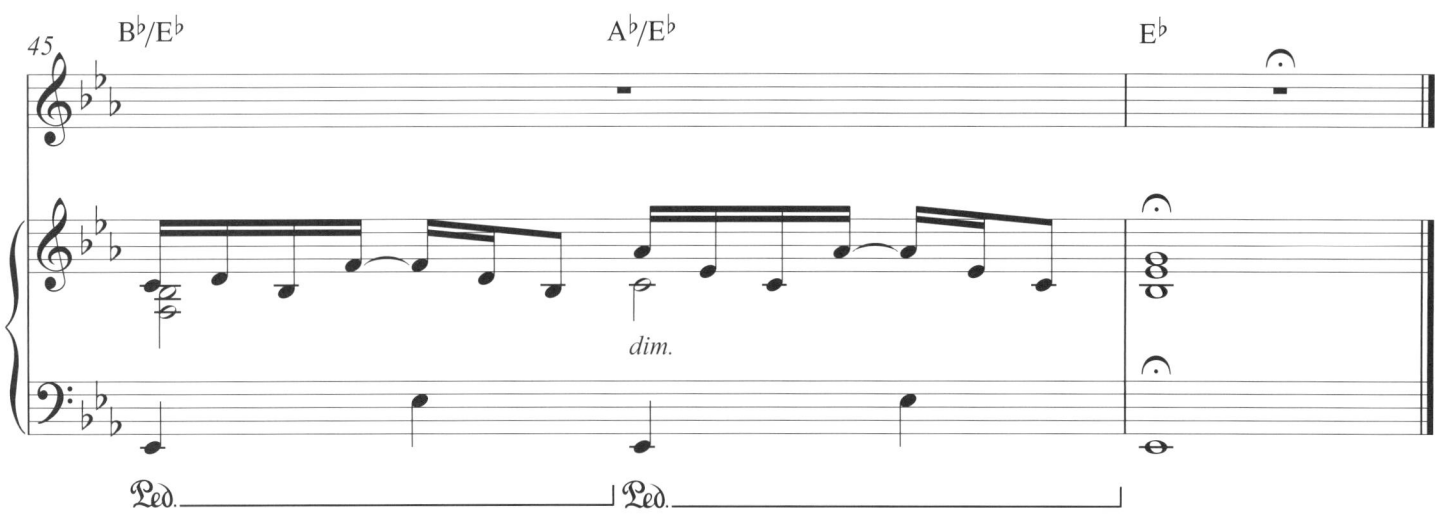

Verse 3:
I sat on the roof and kicked off the moss,
Well a few of the verses, well they've got me quite cross.
But the sun's been quite kind while I wrote this song,
It's for people like you, that keep it turned on.

Verse 4:
So excuse me forgetting but these things I do,
You see, I've forgotten if they're green or they're blue,
Anyway the thing is what I really mean,
Yours are the sweetest eyes I've ever seen.

And you can tell everybody, *etc.*

A THOUSAND MILES
VANESSA CARLTON
GRADE 5 STANDARD

Vanessa Carlton

'A Thousand Miles' was originally started by Vanessa Carlton in 1998 but not finished. The catchy piano riff had hit song written all over it and when Vanessa played it for a record producer years later he told her she had to finish it. She returned home and finished it in one hour, and it became her biggest international hit to date.

Written in B major you have to be very aware of the sharps in this piece. The piano starts alone and it is a great temptation to shorten the tie on beat 3. The examiner will be looking out for this and that the line is controlled in tone. As the piano is solo be very careful of getting ahead of the backing.

There are two distinct techniques in this piece. One is the lyrical line that starts and the other is the punchy, rhythmic episodes. These need a difference in tone.

SONG STATS

Tempo: ♩=94

Key signature: 5 ♯s

The lyrical line needs to be played close to the keys with a warm tone and use of pedal, whilst the rhythmic stabs need to be given weight and accent and a stronger, more strident tone. These chords are played with the backing so make sure you are in sync.

Take note of the crucial rests throughout this piece (for example in bar 5 onward). Also note that this rhythmic work is in the lower register so articulation is very important, particularly in bar 13 which is doubled with the strings.

Throughout this piece there is subtle use of syncopation. Watch the phrase at the end (bars 56–59) and ensure it is evenly maintained.

SUGGESTED LISTENING

Listen to the original recording and notice the delicate energy of Vanessa Carlton's piano playing. Try to apply this feel as you are playing.

43

A THOUSAND MILES

Words & Music by Vanessa Carlton
© Copyright 2001 Rosasharn Publishing/Songs Of Universal Incorporated, USA.
Universal/MCA Music Limited.
All Rights Reserved. International Copyright Secured.

Verse 2:
It's always times like these
When I think of you
And I wonder if you ever think of me.
'Cause everything's so wrong
And I don't belong
Living in your precious memory.
'Cause I need you
And I miss you
And now I wonder:

If I could fall into the sky *etc.*

SONG FOR GUY
ELTON JOHN
GRADE 5 STANDARD

Elon John

Written by Elton John (born Reginald Kenneth Dwight) in 1978, this is one of the most recognisable of his songs. Written primarily for piano, it requires stamina from the performer. On the page, it looks relatively easy, but there are several awkward moments and the examiner will be looking for your attention to detail.

Ensure that you have a singing tone and that the music is played in phrases. The opening is marked moderately loud (*mf*) and means you need to gauge the level of sound to enable you to get louder as the piece progresses to create shape.

With long tied notes throughout, you must be able to balance the sound. The mechanics of the piano mean that once you have struck the note, the sound begins to die away, so you must make sure that the note you play after the tie is not louder. If it is, the music will sound bumpy. Watch that when the percussion enters you are in time.

SONG STATS

Tempo: Moderately

Key signature: No sharps or flats.

There is an element of melody and accompaniment in this piece. An example is bar 8 where the chords are a fill and not part of the melody line. The next section (from bar 17) requires a small glissando effect in the left hand and the examiner will be looking for this so ensure it is smooth. There is some help from the backing here with some strings. Also take note of the rests – they add punch to the line.

Where the line moves up to the upper register, balance the hands to give a clear bell-like sound. The volume should be loud (*f*) here as this is the climax of the song. The initial melody returns (bar 49), but this time as four-note chords, up an octave. This might be too large for some hands – if so, leave out the lowest note but ensure you play the simple octaves.

SUGGESTED LISTENING

Listen to the original recording as well as some of Elton John's live performances – have a go at replicating some of his flamboyance and piano rock feel in your performance.

SONG FOR GUY

Music by Elton John
© Copyright 1978 WAB Publishing Limited.
Universal Music Publishing Limited.
All Rights Reserved. International Copyright Secured.

51

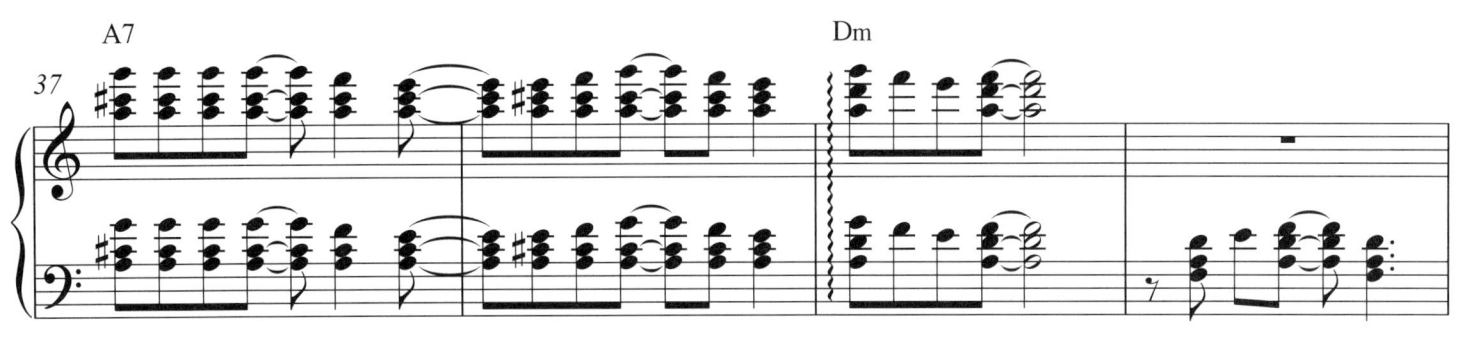
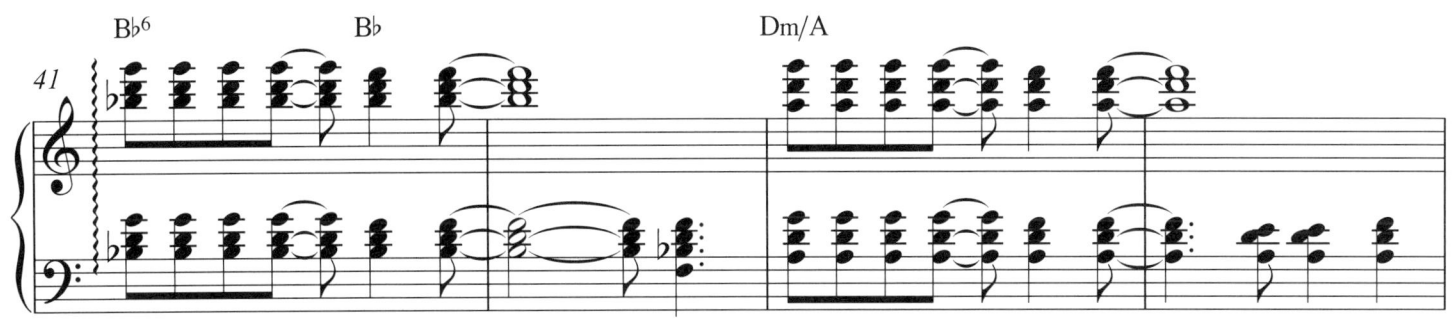
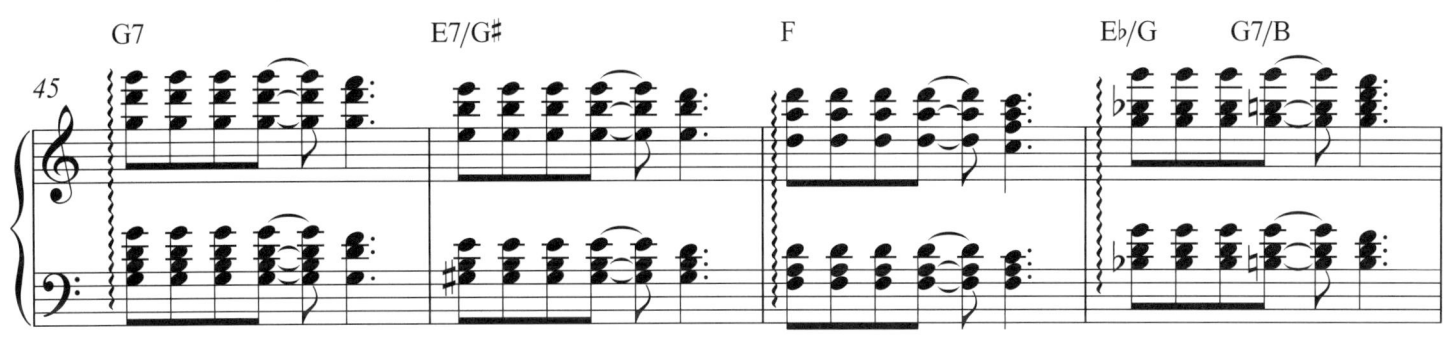
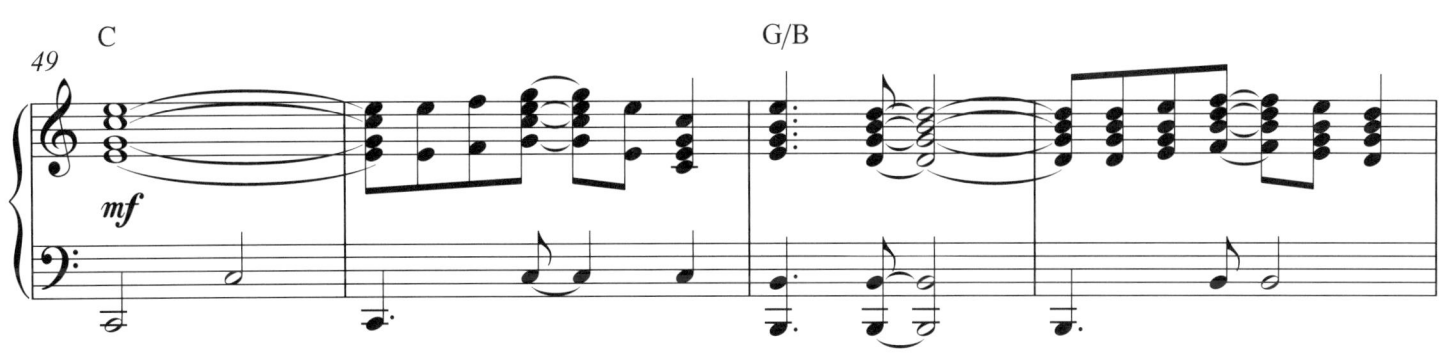
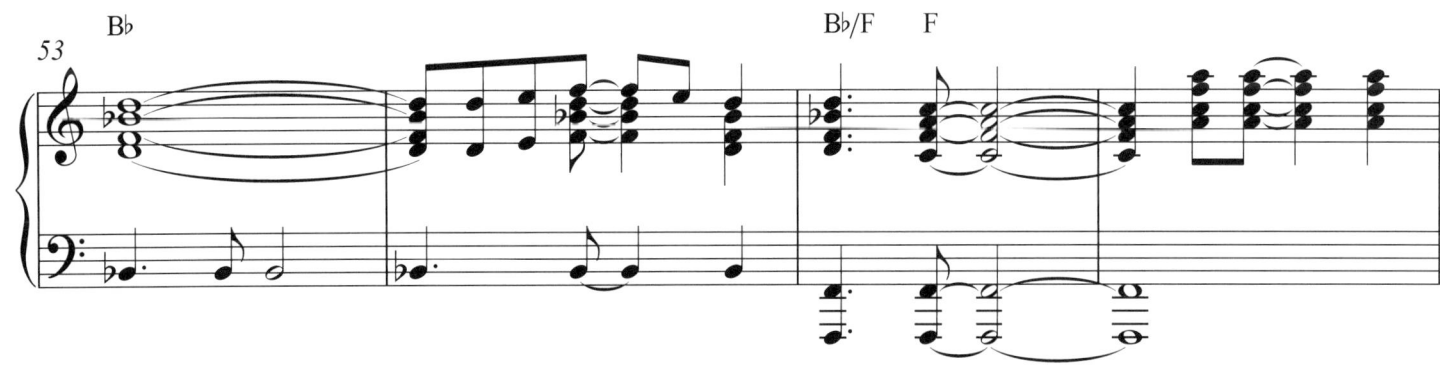

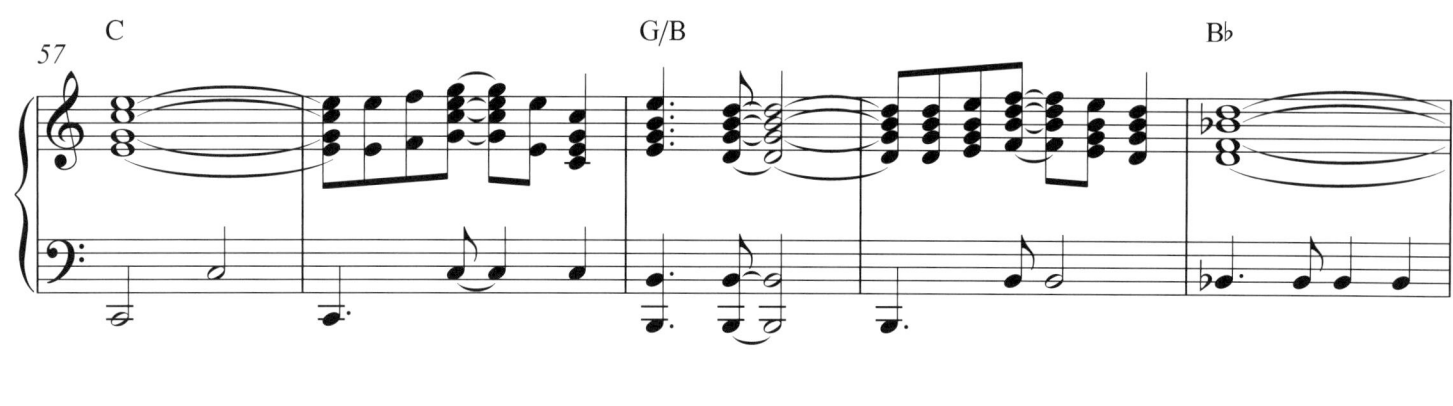

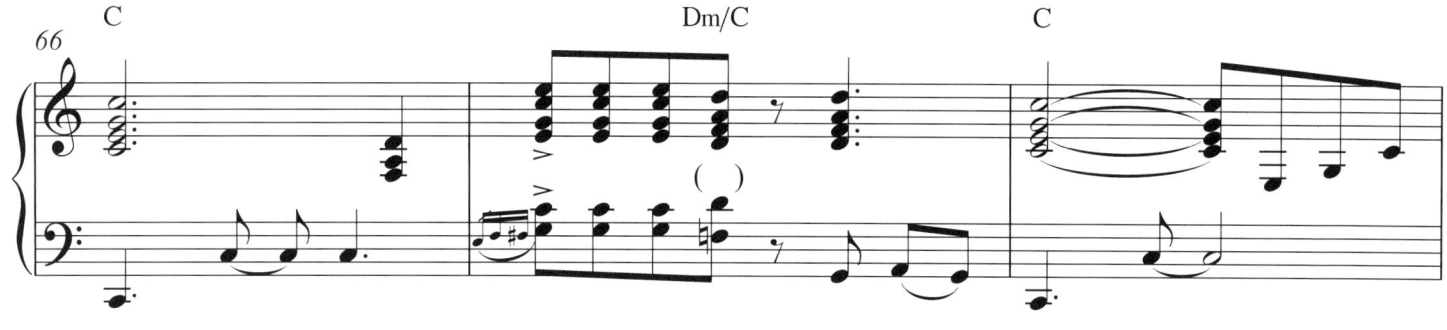

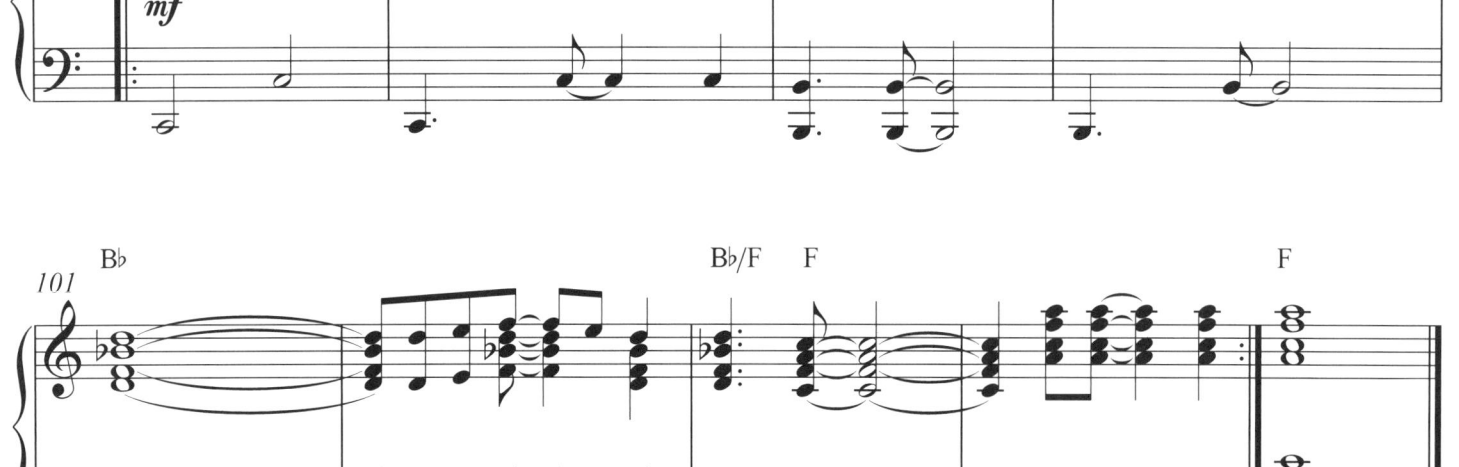

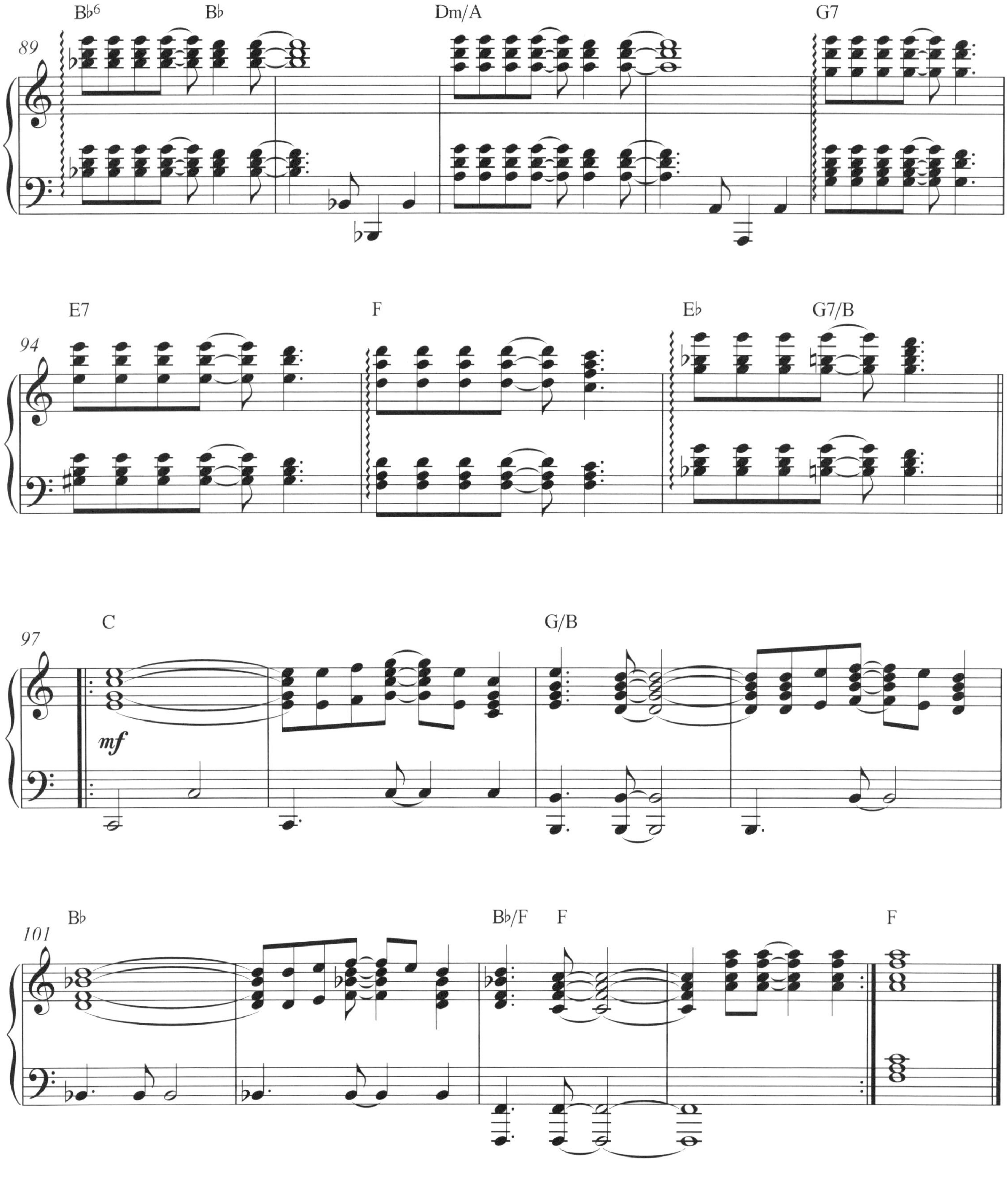
89
B♭6
B♭
Dm/A
G7
94
E7
F
E♭
G7/B
97
C
G/B
mf
101
B♭
B♭/F
F
F

THE WINNER TAKES IT ALL
ABBA
GRADE 5 STANDARD

ABBA

'The Winner Takes It All' was written by Benny Andersson and Bjorn Ulvaeus for ABBA's *Super Trouper* album in 1980. They released it as a single and it has been covered by many international artists since.

The key of this piece is G♭ major, meaning there are six flats. The one to look out for is C♭, as it is the enharmonic equivalent of B. Practise the G♭ major scale a few times before attempting to play the piece. The opening of the song is deceptive, as it feels as if it is on the beat but the melody begins on beat 2. This syncopation is a key part of the whole song and the examiner will be looking out for this. Also you will need to ensure that the long notes in the upper register are held: to do this practise the melody line alone so you can focus on pulling out the main theme.

The left hand line is supportive and it is very important that you emphasise the semitone movement throughout as this is a key harmonic element of the song. You will need to be careful with the pedalling here to make sure you do not blur the harmony.

SONG STATS

Tempo: Steadily

Key signature: 6 ♭s

Also watch that the right hand phrase in bar 1 is shaped with a crescendo into bar 2. Where there are three-note chords make sure that you balance the sound to ensure the upper note sings out (see bar 32).

Enjoy the big chord passage (bar 74-89). If you are unsure of the right hand pitch, it is one octave above the left hand. Note that the left hand is written in the treble clef. Good use of the pedal is needed here. The examiner will be looking for a good balanced dynamic of loud (*f*).

Towards the end, there is a melodic octave phrase in the right hand (from bar 132). Make sure the upper note sings out. Also watch that where there are left hand crotchets, that they are not plodding but are even and sound as a wash of colour rather then individual notes. Stay close to the keys and use the pedal.

SUGGESTED LISTENING

Listen to ABBA's original recording as well as the version sung by actress Meryl Streep for the film *Mamma Mia!* in 2008. This is a dramatic song and is also fun to play, so enjoy it!

THE WINNER TAKES IT ALL

Words & Music by Benny Andersson & Björn Ulvaeus
© Copyright 1980 Union Songs AB, Sweden.
Bocu Music Limited for Great Britain and the Republic of Ireland.
All Rights Reserved. International Copyright Secured.

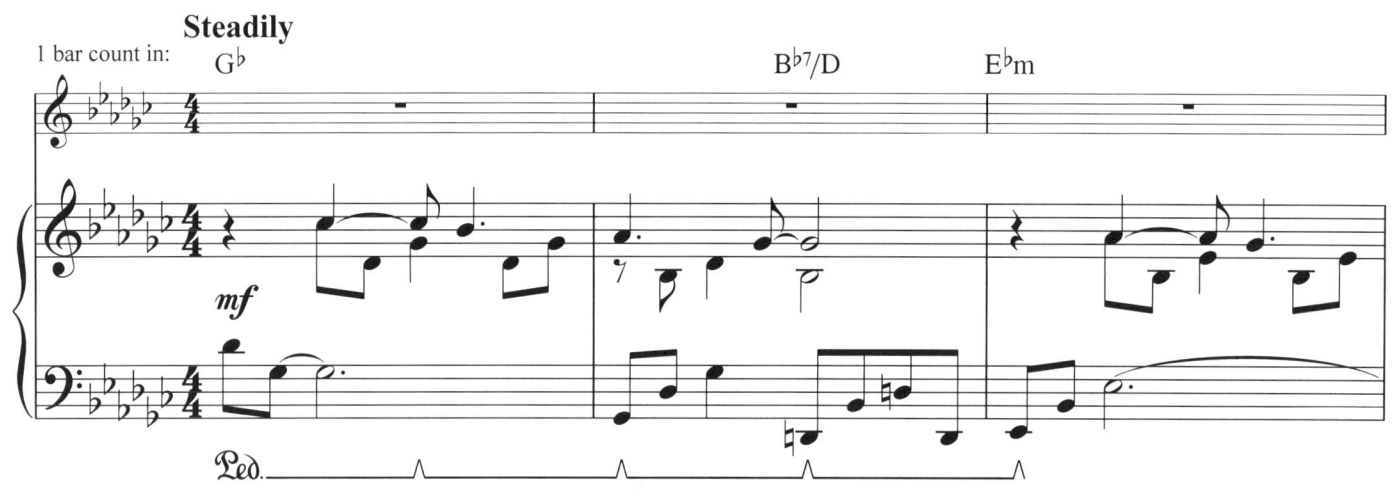

HALO BEYONCÉ
GRADE 6 STANDARD

Beyoncé

It should be noted that this piece, the hardest piece in the book, is beyond the standard you will need for GCSE Music performing. Therefore, play this only if you are totally confident that you really can perform it to the highest standard.

'Halo' was written for the 2008 album *I Am... Sasha Fierce* by Beyoncé. It won Best Female Pop Vocal Performance at the 52nd Grammys and Best Song at 2009 MTV Awards.

The opening chords must be paced to sync with the backing, so spend time listening to this without playing. The semiquaver riff from bar 5 is set against percussion and hand claps. The stresses are not always conventional so listen to the backing and secure the pulse. Pedaling will help the sense of evenness. Watch the ornamentation at the end of bar 6 and ensure it is smoothly incorporated.

SONG STATS
Performance directions: Expressivo

Tempo: ♩=80

Key signature: 3 ♯s

The piano plays the melody line on this track and you must ensure that you balance any chords so the melody line comes through. There is also a lot of syncopation and you need to make sure that the note that follows a tie is no louder than the preceding note. This will help the sense of vocal line (from bar 9).

Where there is rapid repetition of semiquavers on the same pitch, you need to ensure you articulate them clearly (as in bar 11). Do not raise the fingers too far off the keys so you can control the volume.

Your left hand needs to support the right hand with weighted low notes and subtle inner voicing. Where the left hand turns to quavers, these should have a rocking feel but still the lower note should be stronger (from bar 21).

Dynamics are crucial in this piece so make sure you have the range noted from **pp** to **ff**.

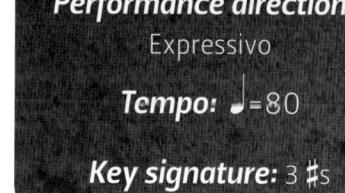

SUGGESTED LISTENING

Listen to the song by Beyoncé, and compare different live versions. Apply some of the same heavy emotion she sings with to your playing for a dramatic performance.

HALO

Words & Music by Ryan Tedder, Beyoncé Knowles & Evan Bogart
© Copyright 2008 Write 2 Live Publishing/Sony/ATV Songs LLC/EMI April Music Incorporated/B Day Publishing, USA.
Kobalt Music Publishing Limited/Sony/ATV Music Publishing/EMI Music Publishing Limited.
All Rights Reserved. International Copyright Secured.

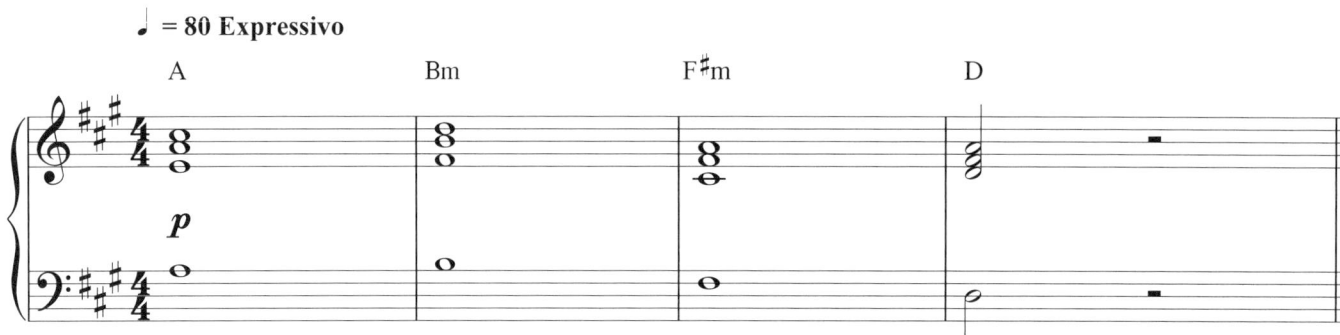

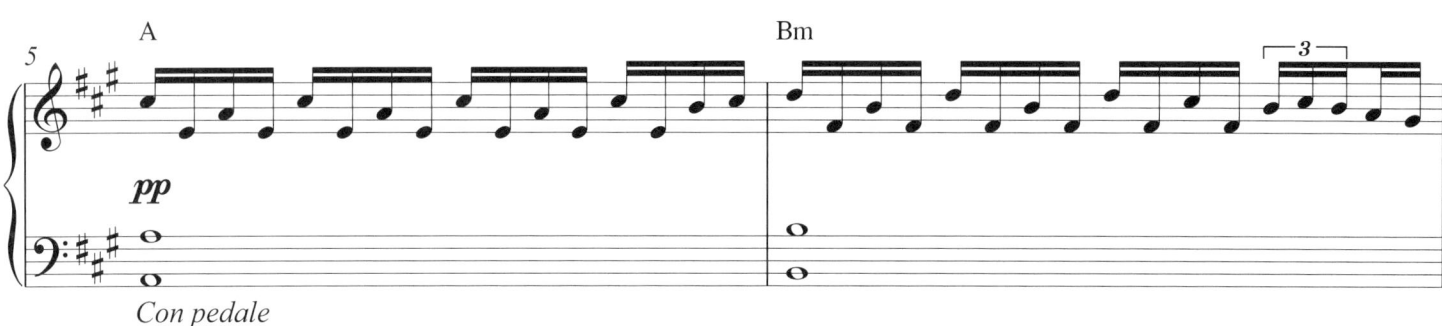

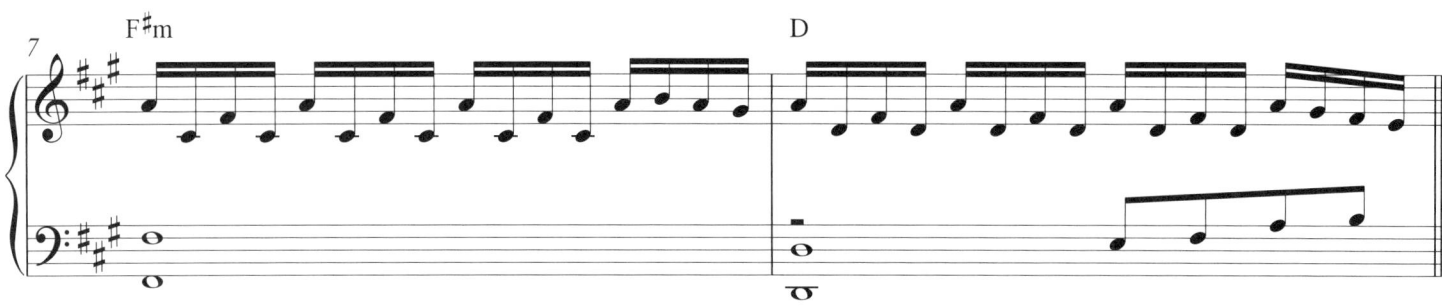

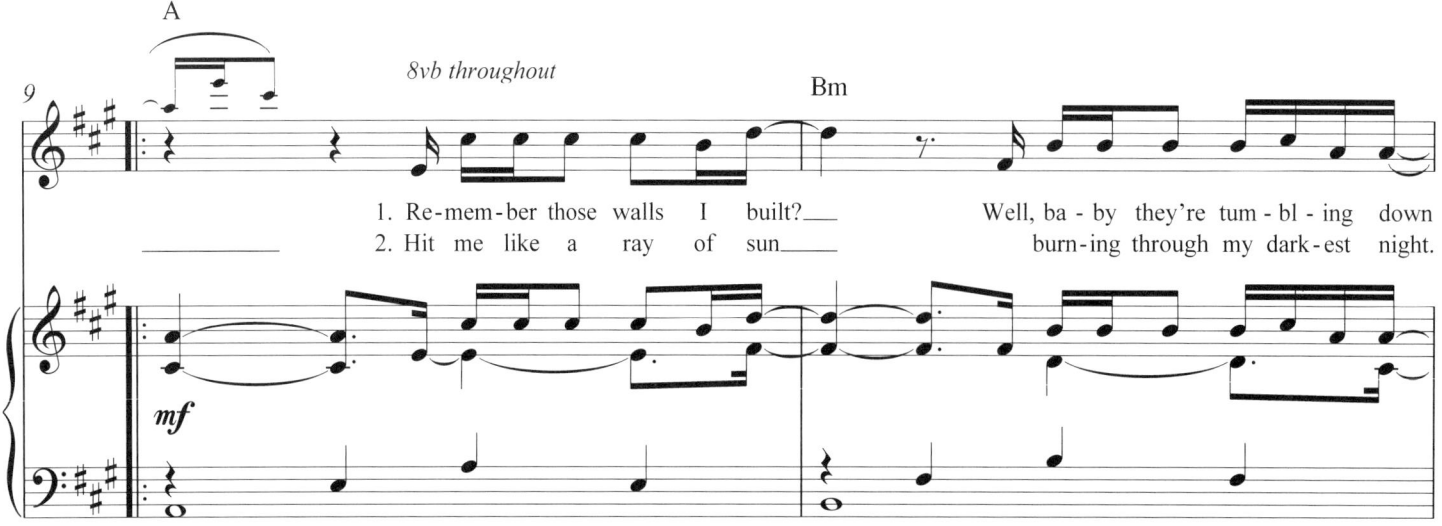

1. Re-mem-ber those walls I built?___ Well, ba-by they're tum-bl-ing down burn-ing through my dark-est night.
2. Hit me like a ray of sun___

A
Bm
42
Ooh.
mf
F♯m
Dadd9
D
44
D.S. al Coda
46
Ev - 'ry - where I'm look - ing now
f
Coda
N.C.
48

1 2 3 4 5 6 7 8 9

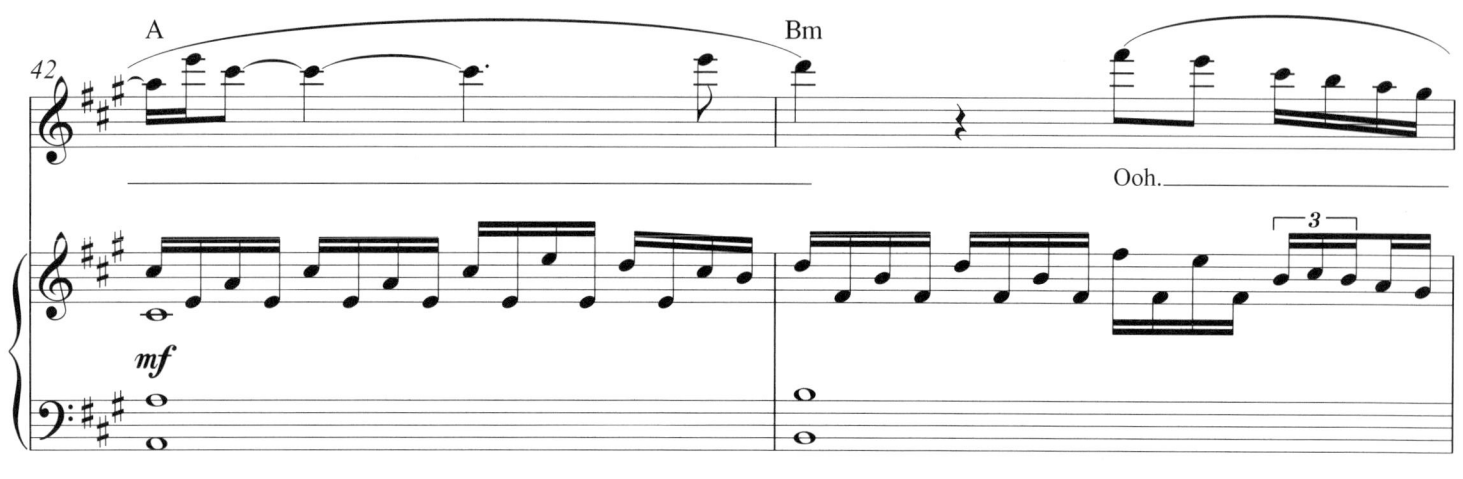

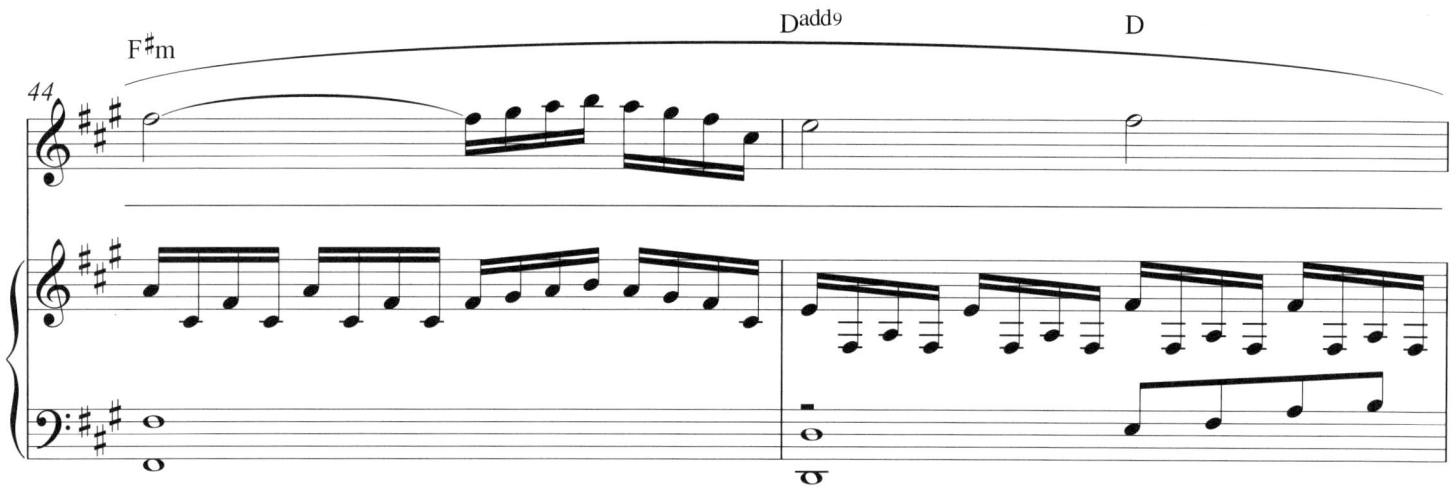

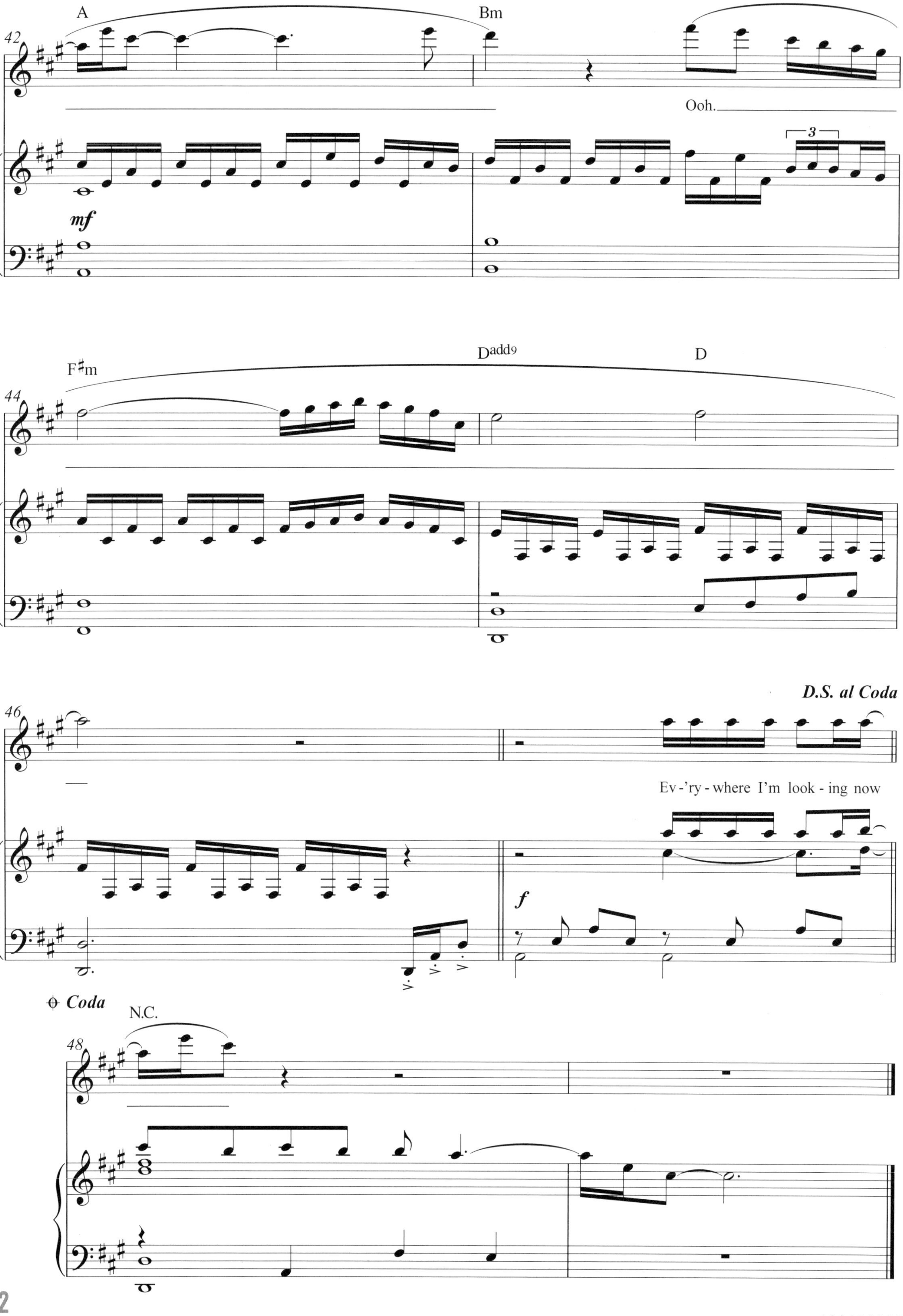